CONTENTS

Air Gracile
Op. 54, No. 1

Alto Saxophone

Anton Dvorak
Arranged by Clair W. Johnson

RUBANK BOOK OF ALTO SAXOPHONE SOLOS
EASY LEVEL

ONLINE MEDIA INCLUDED
Audio Recordings
Printable Piano Accompaniments

PLAYBACK+
Speed • Pitch • Balance • Loop

To access recordings and PDFs of piano accompaniment, visit:
www.halleonard.com/mylibrary

4074-8275-6650-7879

ISBN 978-1-4950-6508-8

RUBANK®

HAL•LEONARD®

Visit Hal Leonard Online at
www.halleonard.com

World headquarters, contact:
Hal Leonard
7777 West Bluemound Road
Milwaukee, WI 53213
Email: info@halleonard.com

In Europe, contact:
Hal Leonard Europe Limited
1 Red Place
London, W1K 6PL
Email: info@halleonardeurope.com

In Australia, contact:
Hal Leonard Australia Pty. Ltd.
4 Lentara Court
Cheltenham, Victoria, 3192 Australia
Email: info@halleonard.com.au

Allerseelen
Op. 10, No. 8

Alto Saxophone

Richard Strauss
Transcribed by Harold L. Walters

At The Hearth

From "Suite Miniature"

Alto Saxophone

A. Gretchaninoff
Transcribed by H. Voxman

Concerto In Bb Minor

Alto Saxophone

Peter I. Tschaikovsky
Transcribed by Herman A. Hummel

Chartreuse

Alto Saxophone

Frank D. Cofield

Alto Saxophone

Danse Arabe

From "The Nutcracker Suite"

Alto Saxophone

Peter I. Tschaikovsky
Arranged by Clarence E. Hurrell

* *Play C with first finger left hand, and middle side key right hand.*

Alto Saxophone

Evening Waltz

From "Suite Miniature"

Alto Saxophone

A. Gretchaninoff
Transcribed by H. Voxman

Tempo di Valse; moderato

Minuet

From "Haffner Music, K. 250"

Alto Saxophone

W. A. Mozart
Transcribed by H. Voxman

Le Secret

Intermezzo

Alto Saxophone

Leonard Gautier
Arranged by Henry W. Davis

Alto Saxophone

TRIO

CODA

Rubank Book of Alto Saxophone Solos – Easy Level
Audio Guide

Selected accompaniment-only recordings include reference "clicks" to
assist the soloist in coordinating entrances, tempo changes, fermatas, etc.
The chart below serves as a guide for using this feature.

Title	Location in printed music	Reference Clicks (Accompaniment-only recording)
At The Hearth *from "Suite Miniature"*	line 1 – **Amoroso**	2 quarters (♩ ♩)
Chartreuse	m. 102 – beat 3 (end of *Cadenza*)	The piano accompaniment re-enters on this beat, followed by two quarter-note clicks in the tempo of m. 103 (**Andante con moto**).
Evening Waltz *from "Suite Miniature"*	line 1 – **Tempo di Valse**	3 quarters (♩ ♩ ♩)
	last line – m. 3, after fermata	2 quarters (♩ ♩)
Minuet *from "Haffner Music," K. 250*	line 1 – **Allegro moderato**	5 quarters (♩ ♩ ♩ ♩ ♩)
	line 6 – **TRIO**	2 quarters (♩ ♩)
	Minuet D.C. al Fine **(Allegro Moderato)**	2 quarters (♩ ♩)